SUPER COOL MECHANICAL ACTIVITIES

WITH MAX AXIOM

by Tammy Enz

Consultant:
Morgan Hynes, Ph.D.
Assistant Professor, Engineering Education
Purdue University
West Lafayette, Indiana

CAPSTONE PRESS
a capstone imprint

Graphic Library is published by Capstone Press,
1710 Roe Crest Drive, North Mankato, Minnesota 56003
www.capstonepub.com

Library of Congress Cataloging-in-Publication Data

Enz, Tammy.
  Super cool mechanical activities with Max Axiom / by Tammy Enz.
      pages cm.—(Graphic library. Max Axiom science and engineering
activities)
  Audience: Ages 8–14.
  Audience: Grade 4 to 6.
  Summary: "Super Scientist, Max Axiom, presents step-by-step
photo-illustrated instructions for building a variety of machines"—
Provided by publisher.
  Includes bibliographical references and index.
  ISBN 978-1-4914-2080-5 (library binding)
  ISBN 978-1-4914-2284-7 (paperback)
  ISBN 978-1-4914-2298-4 (eBook PDF)
1. Mechanical engineering—Juvenile literature. 2. Machinery—Comic
books, strips, etc. 3. Graphic novels. I. Title.
  TJ147.E589 2015
  621—dc23   2014027881

Editor   Project Creation
Christopher L. Harbo   Sarah Schuette and Marcy Morin

Art Director   Photographs by Capstone Studio:
Nathan Gassman   Karon Dubke

Designer
Tracy McCabe

Production Specialist
Katy LaVigne

Cover Illustration
Marcelo Baez

Printed in the United States of
America in Stevens Point,
Wisconsin.
092014   008479WZS15

Table of Contents

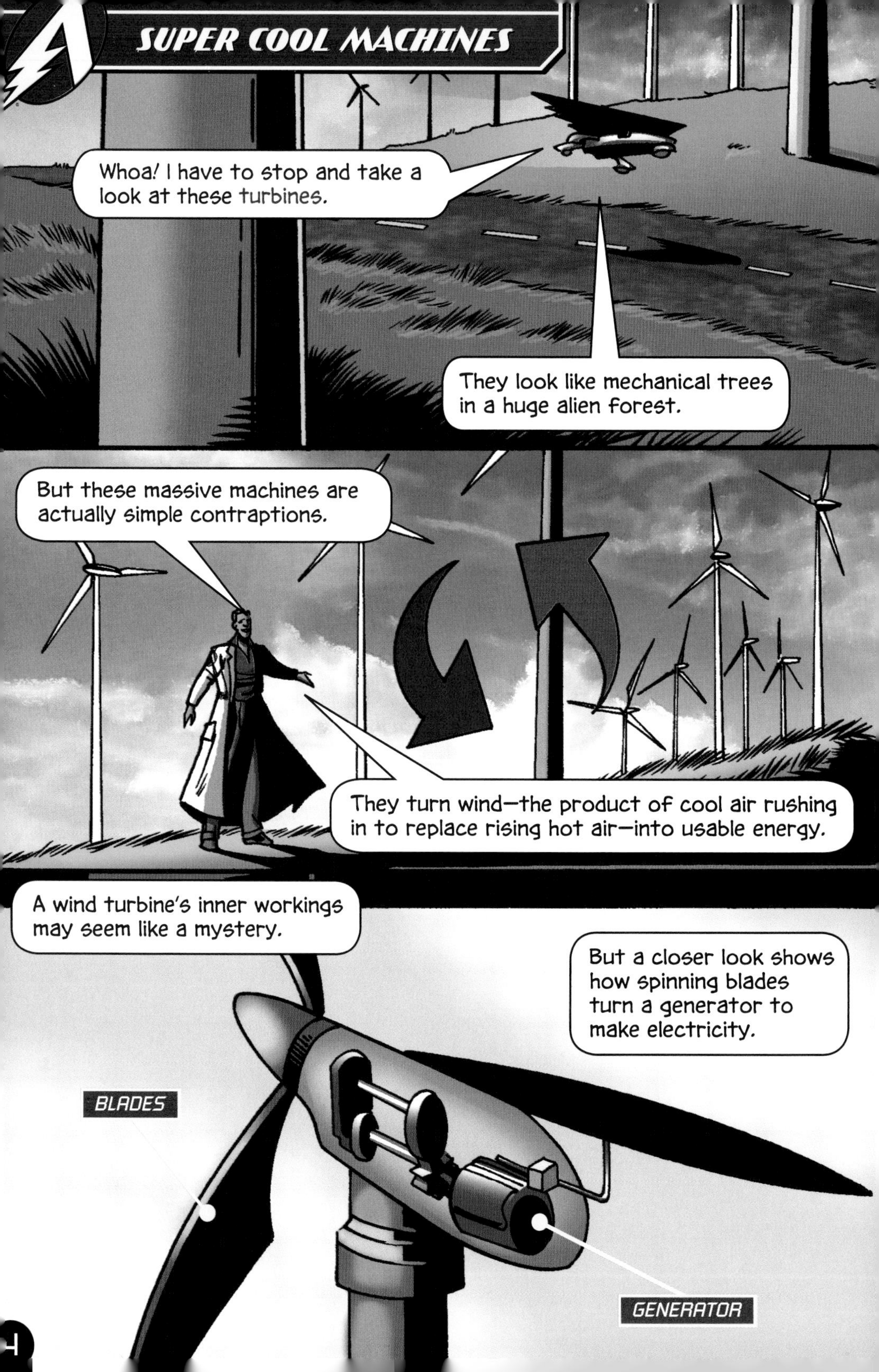
Whoa! I have to stop and take a look at these turbines.
They look like mechanical trees in a huge alien forest.
But these massive machines are actually simple contraptions.
They turn wind—the product of cool air rushing in to replace rising hot air—into usable energy.
A wind turbine's inner workings may seem like a mystery.
But a closer look shows how spinning blades turn a generator to make electricity.
BLADES
GENERATOR

turbine—an engine powered by steam or gas; the steam or gas moves
through the blades of a fanlike device and makes it turn

HOVERCRAFT

Wind turbines aren't the only air-powered machines. This peppy little hovercraft glides across your floor on a cushion of moving air.

YOU'LL NEED

hot glue gun

push-top water bottle cap

old CD

large balloon

SAFETY FIRST

Ask an adult for permission to use a hot glue gun before starting this project.

PLAN OF ACTION

1. Place a bead of hot glue along the bottom edge of the bottle cap. Quickly center the cap over the hole in the CD. Hold it in place for about 15 seconds. Push the top of the cap down to close it.

2. Blow up the balloon and pinch the neck closed to seal in the air. Carefully stretch the mouth of the balloon over the top of the bottle cap.

3. Place the hovercraft on a smooth surface and pull up on the bottle cap's push top to open it. Release the neck of the balloon with a gentle push.

4. Watch the hovercraft sail across the surface on a cushion of air.

AXIOM ALTERNATIVE

Attach the hovercraft horizontally to the back of a small car or set of wheels. See if the machine's backward thrust can push the car forward. Also try cutting fins into a paper plate and using it in place of the CD. Does this change the hover action?

horizontal—flat and parallel to the ground

PULLEY SYSTEM

A pulley is a simple machine made of a wheel turned by a rope or a belt. A pulley system helps lift and move objects. Pulleys change the direction and location of pulling or lifting forces. Try out this system to lift and lower an action figure from across the room.

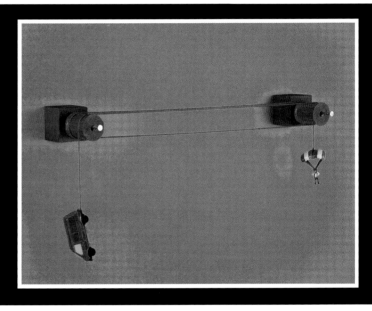

YOU'LL NEED

pencil

4 removable adhesive tabs*

2 2-inch x 2-inch x ¾-inch (5-cm x 5-cm x 2-cm) wood blocks

2 empty thread spools

2 3½-inch- (9-cm-) long nails

hammer

ball of string

scissors

2 small toys

*typically found with adhesive wall hooks

PLAN OF ACTION

1. Ask an adult to help you find an empty wall you can use. Mark two dots at the same height at opposite ends of the wall. At each mark, stick two adhesive tabs with a 1-inch (2.5-cm) gap between them.

2. Place a nail through the center of each spool.

3. Hammer a spool into the center of each of the wooden blocks. Make sure the spools can spin freely.

4. Stick the blocks to adhesive tabs on both ends of the wall.

6. Pull the string under the second spool and guide it back to and around the first spool. Then pull it back to and over the top of the second spool once again.

5. Place the ball of string on the ground under one of the spools. Unwind the string and guide it over the top of this spool. Then carefully pull it to and over the top of the other spool.

7. Let the string hang down to the ground from the second spool. Snip this end of the string off about halfway up the wall.

8. Tie a small toy to each end of the string. Pulling or releasing the figure at either end will do the opposite to the other figure.

⚡ AXIOM ALTERNATIVE

This pulley system has more potential than just lifting objects. See if you can use it to send notes back and forth across the room.

adhesive—a substance, such as glue, that makes things stick together

DIVING SUBMARINE

Submarines use pumps to fill large tanks, called ballasts, with either air or water. Air-filled tanks make the sub more **buoyant** and allow it to float to the surface. When the pumps fill the ballasts with water, the sub becomes less buoyant and sinks below the waves. Make your own submarine to see this action at work.

YOU'LL NEED

plastic drink bottle with a push-top cap

utility knife

2 1-inch- (2.5-cm-) diameter washers

4-foot- (120-cm-) long vinyl hose with an outside dimension of ⅝ inch (16 mm) and an inside dimension of ½ inch (13 mm)

hot glue gun

tub or pool of water

SAFETY FIRST

Ask an adult for permission to use a utility knife and hot glue gun before starting this project.

2. Glue a washer over each of these holes. The washer holes should line up with the bottle's holes.

1. Use the utility knife to carefully cut two holes on one side of the bottle. The holes should be about the size of a pencil eraser and about 3 inches (7.5 cm) apart.

4. Put the submarine in a tub or pool of water with the hose above the water. Watch the submarine sink as water enters its holes. Make it sink faster by gently sucking on the hose.

3. With the bottle cap opened, slide the hose around its tip. Make sure the hose fits tightly. Use hot glue to seal the hose in place if needed.

5. When the submarine is under water, blow into the hose to make it rise to the water's surface.

⚡ AXIOM ALTERNATIVE

Try using a flexible hose and changing the position of the air/water release holes. See if the pump action can move the submarine forward or backward.

PENDULUM PAINTER

A pendulum provides a perfect example of **potential energy** and **kinetic energy** in action. When an object on the end of a string swings upward, it gains potential energy. Gravity then pulls the object downward to change the potential energy to kinetic energy. When the pendulum swings upward again, its energy changes back to potential energy. And so the process repeats. Try using pendulum power to paint some super cool designs.

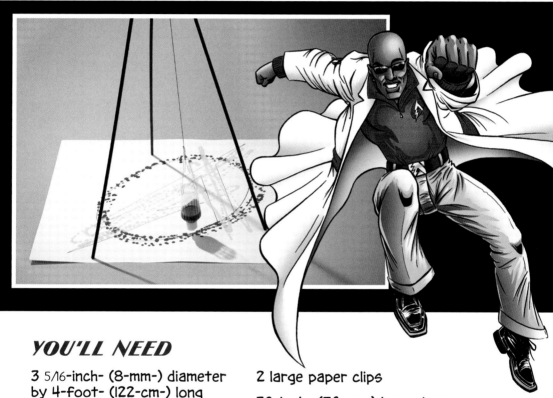

YOU'LL NEED

3 5/16-inch- (8-mm-) diameter by 4-foot- (122-cm-) long wooden dowels

4-foot- (122-cm-) long piece of string

scissors

clean travel size lotion bottle with lid

large sewing needle

2 large paper clips

30-inch- (76-cm-) long piece of string

washable poster paint

water

coffee stir stick

large sheets of paper

1. Arrange the dowels to form a tripod with legs about 2 feet (0.6 m) apart. Let the tops of the dowels cross each other and overlap by about 4 inches (10 cm).

2. Wrap the 4-foot (1.2-m) string tightly around and under the crossing dowels. Continue wrapping until the tripod is tightly bound and its legs stay in position. Tie off the ends of the string.

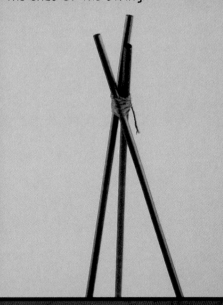

3. Cut off the bottom of the lotion bottle with a scissors.

4. Use the needle to poke two holes on opposite sides of the bottle about 1/2 inch (1 cm) from the open end.

potential energy—the stored energy of an object that is raised, stretched, or squeezed

kinetic energy—the energy of a moving object

continued

of the paper clips. Both paper clips will now have bends on each end.

6. Clip one end of each paper clip through a hole in the lotion bottle.

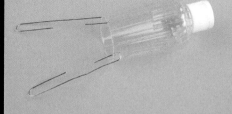

7. Tie a 1-inch (2.5-cm) loop in one end of the 30-inch (76-cm) piece of string. Tie the other end around the tripod top, leaving the loop hanging down.

8. Clip the paper clip hooks to the loop.

9. With the lid closed, fill the lotion bottle about one-third full with poster paint. Fill another third of the bottle with water. Use the stir stick to mix the paint.

10. Position a large sheet of paper under the painter. Carefully open the cap. Swing and twirl the bottle to watch the pendulum paint a design on the paper.

AXIOM ALTERNATIVE

Try attaching a second string and bottle with a different color paint. Swing the bottles at the same time to create an even more colorful painting. Try using different lengths of string to see how the design changes.

PUMP DRILL

A pump drill is an ancient tool still used today. It uses **momentum** created by the spinning motion of a disc placed on a shaft to create a drilling motion. See this amazing pump drill in action for yourself!

YOU'LL NEED

¾-inch (19-mm) x 18-inch (46-cm) wooden dowel

wood saw

2-inch (5-cm) nail

hammer

wire snips

5½-inch x 1½-inch x ¾-inch (14-cm x 4-cm x 2-cm) block of wood

drill

⅞-inch (22-mm) drill bit

⅛-inch (3-mm) drill bit

30-inch- (76-cm-) long piece of string

large plastic coffee can lid

utility knife

electrical tape

piece of scrap wood

SAFETY FIRST

Ask an adult for help when asked to use a drill, saw, or utility knife for this project.

momentum—the amount of motion an object carries

continued

PLAN OF ACTION

1. Cut a ½-inch (2-cm) deep slit in one end of the dowel with the saw.

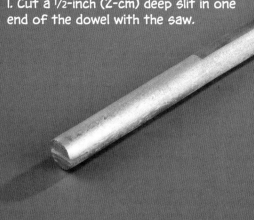

2. Pound the nail into the center of the other end of the dowel with the hammer. Leave about 1 inch (3 cm) of the nail sticking out. Snip off the head of the nail with the wire snips.

3. Drill a hole into the center of the small piece of wood with the 7/8-inch (22-mm) drill bit.

4. Drill two small holes in the piece of wood with the 1/8-inch (3-mm) drill bit. Each hole should be centered about ½ inch (2 cm) from the ends of the wood.

5. Thread one end of the string through one of the small holes. Knot the end. Repeat this step with the other end of the string and the second small hole. Make sure the knots are large enough so they do not slip through the holes.

6. Slide the dowel through the large hole. Insert the string through the slit in the dowel.

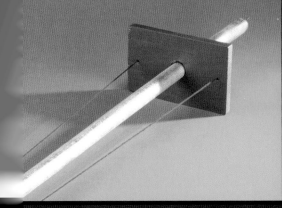

7. Cut a hole through the center of the coffee can lid with the utility knife. Make the hole just large enough so the dowel fits snugly through it.

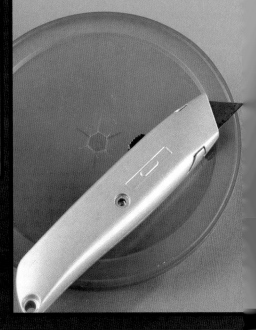

8. Slide the lid up the dowel so that it rests just below the piece of wood hanging on the string. Tape the lid in place.

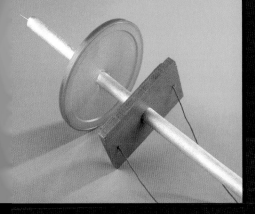

9. Wrap the string around the dowel a few times by turning the piece of wood. Position the pump drill's nail on a piece of scrap wood. Start drilling by pushing the pump drill's wood handle downward. Allow momentum to pull the handle back up before pushing it down again. This momentum will cause the dowel to spin and the nail to drill a hole.

⚡ AXIOM ALTERNATIVE

Experiment with different drill bits. Try using a screw instead of a nail for better precision or for drilling a larger hole.

TREBUCHET

A trebuchet was a weapon used in the Middle Ages. This mechanical throwing device uses gravity's pull on a **counterweight** to fling an object. In a few simple steps, your trebuchet will fling marbles across the room.

YOU'LL NEED

8 large wooden craft sticks

ruler

hot glue gun

2 wooden chopsticks

rubber band

plastic drink bottle cap

drill

1/8-inch (3-mm) drill bit

masking tape

4 1-inch- (2.5-cm-) diameter washers

marble

SAFETY FIRST

Ask an adult for permission to use a hot glue gun and drill before starting this project.

1. Lay three craft sticks out to form a triangle. Overlap their ends so that the ends are flush at two points of the triangle. At the third point, they should overlap each other by 1 inch (3 cm). Glue the sticks in this position.

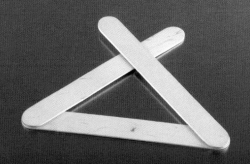

2. Repeat step 1 with three more sticks.

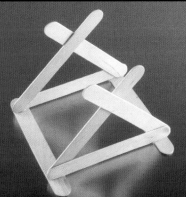

3. Lay the remaining two sticks parallel to each other and about 5 inches (13 cm) apart. Straddle the sticks with the flush sides of the upright triangles, placing them about 4 inches (10 cm) apart. Glue them in place.

4. Form a cross with the chopsticks. Wind the rubber band tightly around the cross to hold the pieces together.

counterweight—a weight that balances a load

flush—exactly even

5. Drill a hole in the side of the plastic cap. Slide one end of one chopstick into it. Secure with glue.

6. On the other end of the chopstick with the cap, wrap several layers of masking tape. Slide the washers over the masking tape, making sure they fit very snugly.

7. Set the arms of the cross over the triangle supports. Adjust the rubber band so the washers can swing freely below the crossbar.

8. Pull the cap back and place a marble in it. Release the lid to fling the marble.

⚡ AXIOM ALTERNATIVE

Some trebuchets used a sling instead of a fixed basket. Try replacing the cap with a sling for flinging the marble.

HYDRO-POWERED WINCH

Moving water is a powerful force. Falling water can turn a wheel to generate electricity, run a sawmill, or grind grain. With just a few household supplies, you can build a water wheel winch.

YOU'LL NEED

empty 2-liter bottle

ruler

pencil

utility knife

2 small binder clips

2 thin plastic container lids

scissors

chopstick

12-inch (30-cm) piece of string

tape

small toy

pitcher

water

SAFETY FIRST

Ask an adult for help when asked to use a utility knife for this project.

1. Measure 7 inches (18 cm) up from the bottom of the 2-liter bottle. Mark a line all around the bottle at this height. Carefully cut along this line with the utility knife to remove the top of the bottle.

2. Set the bottle top upside down inside the bottom of the bottle. Clip the binder clips opposite from each other along the edge of the bottle top. Flip the inside handles of the binder clips down.

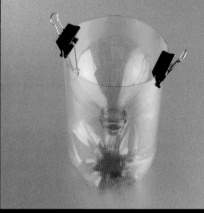

3. Measure and cut two 2¾-inch x 3-inch (70-mm x 76-mm) rectangles from the centers of the plastic lids.

4. Fold one piece of plastic in half along the short dimension.

5. Measure and mark lines every ½ inch (13 mm) along the folded edge.

6. Use a scissors to cut short slits at each mark.

7. Repeat steps 4 through 6 with the other plastic piece.

8. Unfold the rectangles and lay them back-to-back so their slits line up. Weave the chopstick through the slits in both pieces of plastic to hold them together. Spread the four plastic flaps apart to create a water wheel.

9. Slide the chopstick ends through the handles on the binder clips.

10. Tie and tape the string to the longer side of the chopstick. Tie the toy to the end of the string.

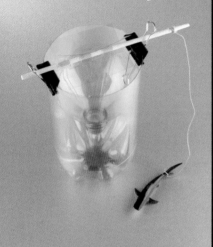

11. Gently pour water from the pitcher onto the center of one of the paddles to turn the winch. As the winch turns it will lift the toy.

⚡ AXIOM ALTERNATIVE

Apply moving air to the paddles with a hair dryer. You'll convert the winch from hydropower to wind power. Which has more lifting power, wind or water?

HYDRAULIC ARM

Heavy machinery and many mechanical devices use hydraulic power. Hydraulics use pressurized fluid to lift, push, pull, and dig. Experiment with the power of hydraulics with a simple hydraulic digging arm project.

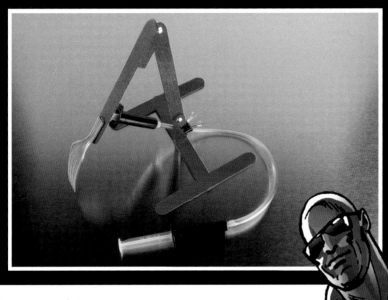

YOU'LL NEED

6 large wooden craft sticks

ruler

hot glue gun

pencil

drill

1/8-inch (3-mm) drill bit

2 brass fasteners

plastic fork

2 syringes

heavy duty shears

12-inch- (30-cm-) long plastic hose with a 1/8-inch (3-mm) inside diameter

small binder clip

SAFETY FIRST

Ask an adult for permission to use a hot glue gun and drill before starting this project.

PLAN OF ACTION

1. Place two craft sticks parallel to each other. Their outside edges should be about 6 inches (15 cm) apart.

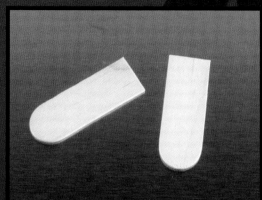

3. Measure and mark a line 2 inches (5 cm) from each end of another stick. Use the shears to cut along each of these lines. Discard the center portion.

5. Repeat step 4 with the remaining 2-inch (5-cm) piece.

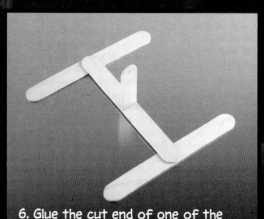

6. Glue the cut end of one of the 2-inch (5-cm) pieces to the center of the H created in step 2. The piece should stand straight up.

2. Place a drop of hot glue on the center of each stick. Place another stick across the first two to form a letter H. Hold it to the hot glue for about 15 seconds.

4. On one of the 2-inch (5-cm) pieces, measure and mark a dot 1/4-inch (6-mm) down from the center of the rounded end. Drill a hole at this dot.

7. Glue one edge of the other 2-inch (5-cm) piece to the center of the flat side of another craft stick. Line up their rounded ends

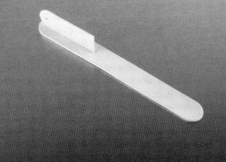

continued

8. On the remaining stick, measure and mark a dot 1/4 inch (6 mm) from the center of each rounded end. Drill holes at each dot.

9. Line up the holes in the long stick with the holes in each of the 2-inch (5-cm) pieces. Connect the pieces with the brass fasteners.

10. Use the shears to cut the handle off the fork and discard it. Glue the fork head, tines down, to the top of the digging arm. The fork should extend off the end of the arm.

11. Insert each of the syringe tips into either end of the hose. Remove one of the syringe's plungers. Close the other syringe's plunger.

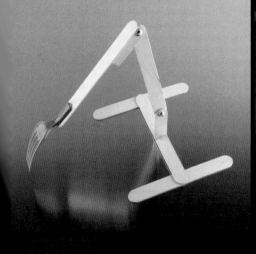

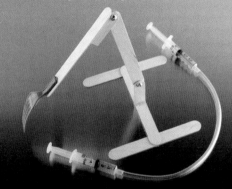

12. With help from a friend, fill the empty plunger with water, pulling the other plunger to fill the hose and syringe. Replace the first plunger. Adjust the syringes so that as one opens, the other closes.

13. Glue the end of one of the plungers to the bottom of the digging arm.

14. Secure the hose to the upright stick with the binder clip. Adjust its location so the arm swings easily up and down when the plunger on the unsecured syringe is pushed or pulled.

AXIOM ALTERNATIVE

For better digging action, try adding a bending joint where the fork attaches to the machine. You can also replace the fork with a spoon for lifting objects, or try adding a paintbrush for painting a design.

ELECTRIC FAN MOTOR

Most motors hide inside the machines they run. But if you could peel back the layers, you'd see an amazingly simple concept at work. Motors use the attracting and repelling properties of magnets to their advantage. An electric current in a loop of wire creates a magnetic field that spins when it is near a magnet. Witness this concept in action by building your own motor-powered fan.

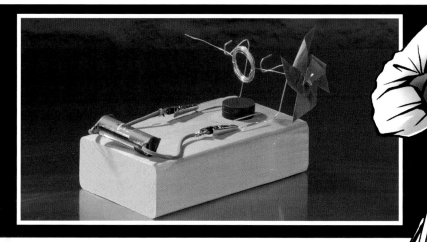

YOU'LL NEED

5 feet (1.5 m) of enamel-coated magnet wire

broom

sandpaper

1½-inch (4-cm) square of paper

scissors

hot glue gun

sewing needle

2 large metal paper clips

needle-nosed pliers

6-inch- (15-cm-) long 2 x 4 board

heavy duty stapler

3 1-inch- (2.5-cm) diameter circular magnets

2 5-inch- (13-cm-) long plastic coated electrical wires

wire-stripping tool

2 small alligator clips

electrical tape

AA battery

SAFETY FIRST

Ask an adult for permission to use a hot glue gun before starting this project.

PLAN OF ACTION

1. Wind the enamel-coated wire around the broom handle at least 15 times. Leave 2 inches (5 cm) loose at each end. Wrap each end twice around the coil on opposite sides to hold the coils together.

2. Use the sandpaper to sand off all the enamel on one of the 2-inch (5-cm) ends. Sand only one side of the enamel off the other 2-inch (5-cm) end.

3. Cut diagonal slits almost to the center from each corner of the paper.

4. Bend the corner of every other paper flap into the center of the paper. Hot glue the corners to the center to make fan blades.

5. Use the needle to punch a hole through the center of the dried hot glue. Stick one end of the coiled wire into the hole on the back side of the fan.

6. Bend one loop of a paper clip at a 90-degree angle. Use the pliers to kink the end of this loop into a small S shape. Repeat with the other paper clip.

7. Staple the unkinked loops of the paper clips about 2½ inches (6 cm) apart near one end of the 2 x 4.

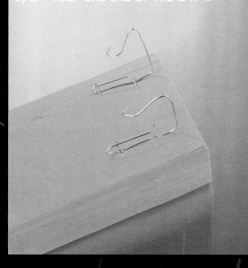

8. Place the wire coil across the paper clip supports. Stack the magnets under the coils.

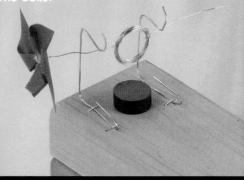

10. Clip each alligator clip to one end of the stapled paper clips. Tape their other ends to opposite sides of the battery.

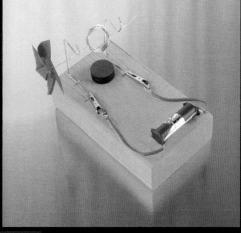

9. Strip about 1 inch (3 cm) of coating from each end of one of the coated wires. Attach an alligator clip to one end. Repeat with the other wire.

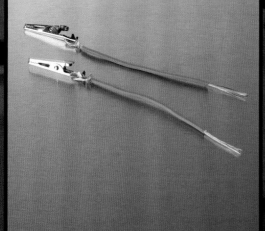

11. Gently flick the wire coil to start it rotating. The fan will begin turning. It can be stopped by unclipping one of the alligator clips.

⚡ AXIOM ALTERNATIVE

Try replacing the battery with a hobby-size solar cell to run the motor using an alternate energy source.

Glossary

adhesive (ad-HEE-siv)—a substance, such as glue, that makes things stick together

buoyant (BOI-uhnt)—able to keep afloat

counterweight (KAUN-tuhr-wayt)—a weight that balances a load

dimension (duh-MEN-shuhn)—an object's measurement or size; an object's dimensions are length, width, and height

flush (FLUSH)—exactly even

horizontal (hor-uh-ZON-tuhl)—flat and parallel to the ground

kinetic energy (ki-NET-ik EN-ur-jee)—the energy of a moving object

momentum (moh-MEN-tuhm)—the amount of motion an object carries

potential energy (puh-TEN-shuhl EN-ur-jee)—the stored energy of an object that is raised, stretched, or squeezed

turbine (TUR-bine)—an engine powered by steam or gas; the steam or gas moves through the blades of a fanlike device and makes it turn

Read More

Enz, Tammy. *Zoom It: Invent New Machines that Move.* Invent It. Mankato, Minn.: Capstone Press, 2012.

Meachen Rau, Dana. *Simple Machines.* A True Book. New York: Children's Press, 2012.

Rissman, Rebecca. *Simple Machines.* Real Size Science. Chicago: Capstone Heinemann Library, 2013.

Internet Sites

FactHound offers a safe, fun way to find Internet sites related to this book. All of the sites on FactHound have been researched by our staff.

Here's all you do:

Visit *www.facthound.com*

Type in this code: 9781491420805

 **Super-cool stuff!** Check out projects, games and lots more at **www.capstonekids.com**

Index